ANIMAL MANDALA
COLORING BOOK
FOR ALL AGES
JIM STEPHENS

All Rights reserved. No part of this book may be reproduced or used in any way or form or by any means whether electronic or mechanical, this means that you cannot record or photocopy any material ideas or tips that are provided in this book.

© [2016] Jim Stephens

ISBN 978-0692655757

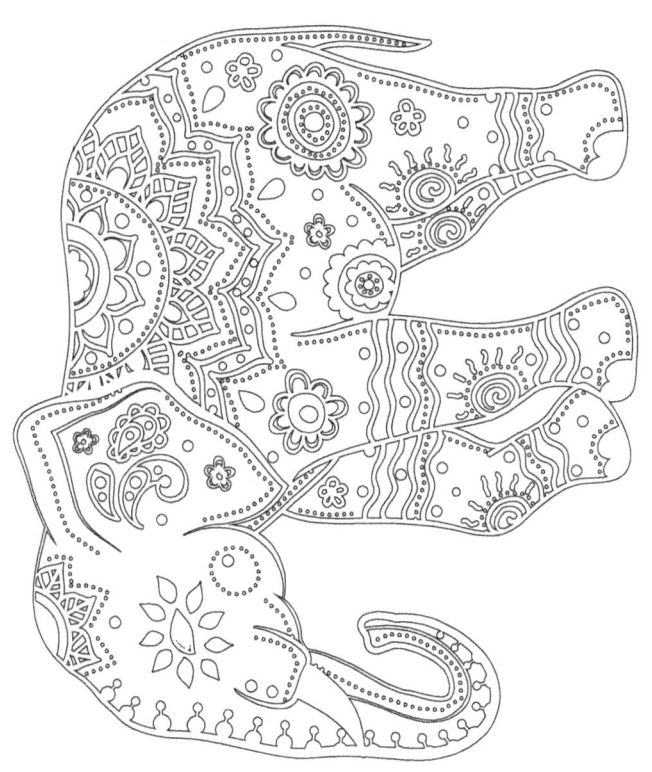

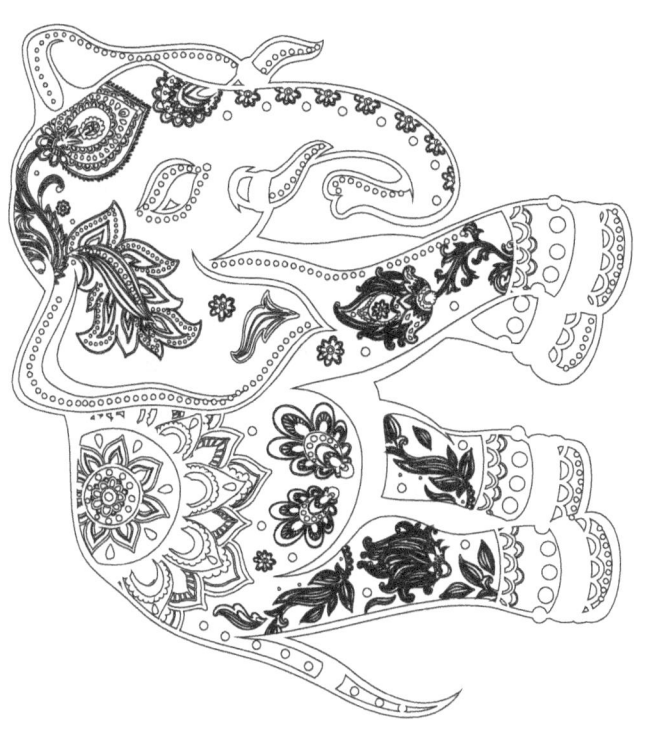

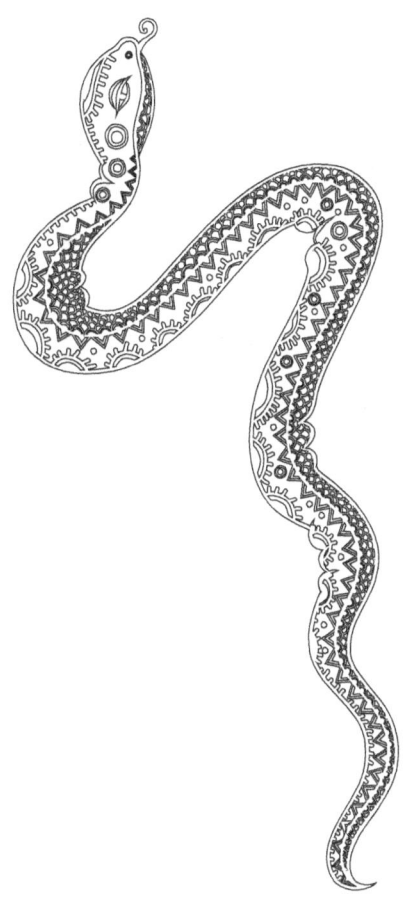

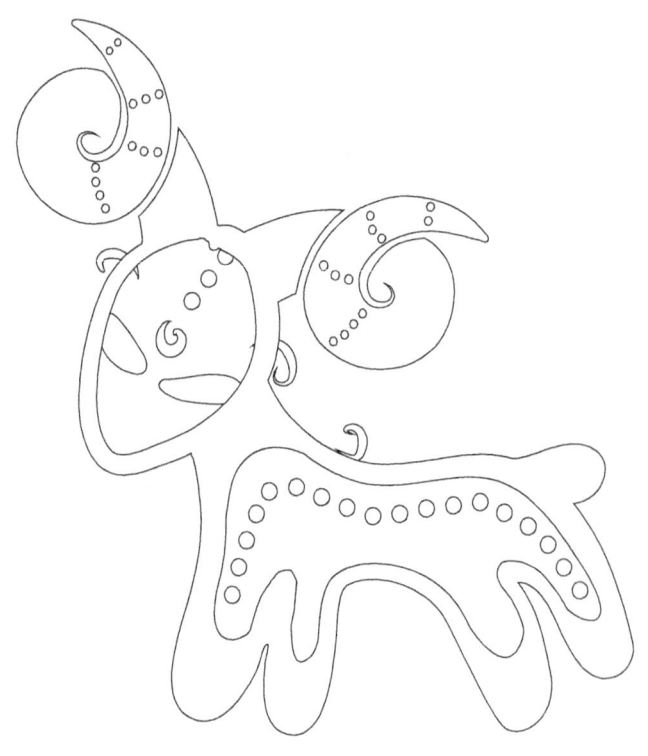

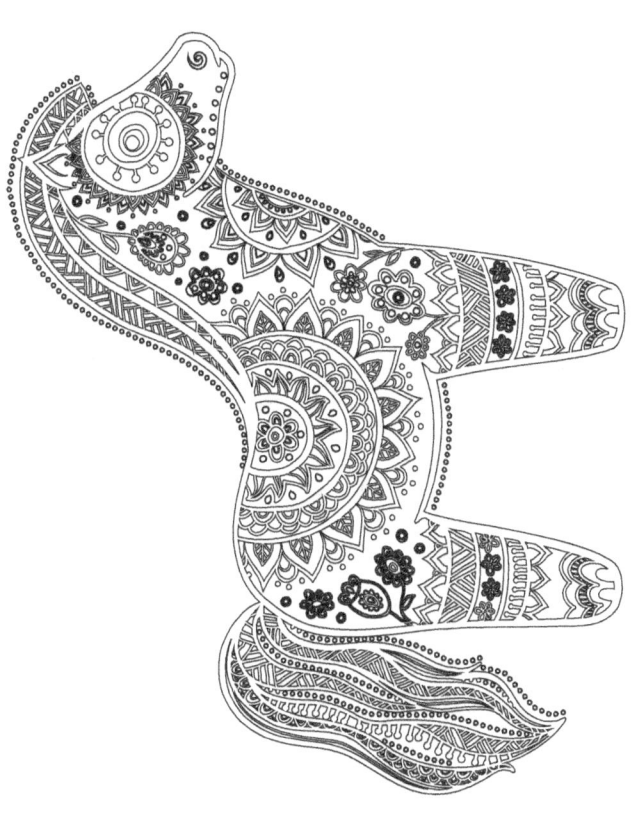

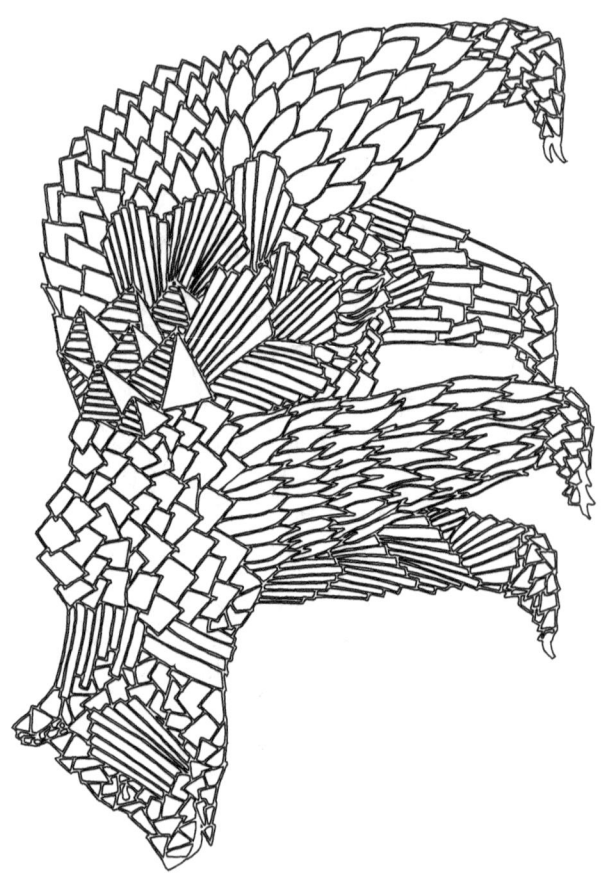

www.ingramcontent.com/pod-product-compliance
Lightning Source LLC
Chambersburg PA
CBHW072113290426
44110CB00014B/1902